My Entrepreneur Journal

A Daily Practice for Achieving Success and Abundance

Simple Journals by Vanessa Marie Dewsbury

ISBN: 978-1-7751949-2-7

THIS JOURNAL BELONGS TO

Welcome to My Entrepreneur Journal for Achieving Success and Abundance.

The intention of this 90-day journal is to encourage, motivate, and inspire you to achieve your goals and dreams in your personal and professional life. The purpose of this journal is to help you connect within to where your true power and confidence resides.

Each page contains the following:

- Daily Gratitude
- Empowering Affirmation
- Self-Care
- Intention Setting
- Goals
- Self-Reflection

I suggest writing a note to yourself committing to taking the time each day to engage in this daily practice. The more consistent you are with your daily routines, the more successful you will be, and become.

Enjoy and have fun!

Benefits of Journaling

- Journaling gives you a sense of accomplishment, which helps build your confidence and self-esteem
- Helps you create new habits that will result in greater productivity and self-discipline
- Assists you in connecting deeper to your creative and inspirational energies
- Allows you time for self-reflection and helps you track your progress and growth
- Slows you down so you can organize your thoughts, goals, and intentions
- Gives you the opportunity to connect to your emotions

Benefits of Gratitude

- Daily gratitude contributes to a healthy sense of well-being and self-awareness
- Encourages you to be thankful for all the beautiful things in your life
- Helps lower stress levels which keeps you balanced and grounded
- Assists in strengthening the relationships with yourself and with others
- Helps increase your feelings of optimism, inspiration, and motivation
- Keeps you open to the abundance and prosperity that is available to you

Benefits of Self-Reflection

- Self-Reflection helps bring new levels of self-awareness and perspective, which contributes to healing and growth
- Helps you define your purpose, your potential, and your passions
- Allows you to identify what matters most in your life and business
- Creates a stronger sense of inner connection
- Assists you in recognizing any areas that may need a little more work
- Helps you see your unique gifts, talents, and your greatest abilities

Benefits Of Affirmations

- Affirmations are known to stimulate neural activities which promotes internal change
- They help you develop a healthy, abundant, and balanced mindset
- Improves your mood and can shift you from a negative to a positive state of mind
- Quiets your inner critic as you take control of your own thoughts and feelings
- Calms your anxiety and nervous system when used during stressful moments
- Enhances your self-esteem, self-confidence, and self-worth

Benefits of Setting Goals

- Setting goals helps you better manage your time, energy, and focus
- You are more likely to achieve your goals when you write them down
- Helps you measure your daily progress and growth
- Assists you in getting crystal clear on what you desire
- Encourages you to visualize your future as you work on building your business
- Improves your mental health and increases your level of personal and professional success

Benefits of Setting Intentions

- Setting daily intentions keeps you grounded and balanced in the present moment
- Helps you stay connected to your why and keeps you focused on your goals
- Reminds you of your purpose as you create and build your dreams
- Acts as a powerful map to your desires and future destination
- Leads to a positive and productive state of mind
- Encourages you to stay mindful and aware on your journey of growth and self-development

Difference between goals and intentions

Goals are focused on future, external accomplishments (what you want to do – finish a half marathon), while intentions are focused on the present internal state of being (how you want to be or feel in the moment – happy, healthy, at peace).

Benefits of Self-Care

- Self-Care improves one's overall sense of well-being and feelings of worthiness
- Helps you recognize your value and importance in the world
- Reduces stress and anxiety when you take the time to take care of your own needs
- Builds a strong sense of self and keeps you balanced mentally, emotionally, spiritually, and physically
- Relaxes your neurological system which helps with better sleep and digestion
- Improves your focus and brings you a deeper sense of calm, clarity, and connection

Every accomplishment is
a small step toward big success.

Affirmations for Success & Abundance

Allow your intuition to guide you as you choose a new Empowering Affirmation each day from the list' below.

o   I am worthy of manifesting my dreams and my desires.

o   I believe in myself and my ability to succeed.

o   Something wonderful is about to happen and I am open and ready to receive.

o   I allow love to fill me up and guide me in all my actions.

o   Everything is always working out for me as I stay aligned with my goals and my dreams.

o   My mind is free of resistance and open to brand new possibilities and opportunities.

o   I am in the process of becoming the very best version of myself.

o   I look for the good in all situations and I learn and grow from all my experiences.

o   My dreams and desires are fueled by an unlimited belief in myself.

o   I know I can do absolutely anything I put my heart and mind to.

o   I have faith in myself and in my unique talents and abilities.

o   I have whatever it takes to reach my goals and my truest desires.

o   I am strong enough to overcome any obstacle that comes my way.

o   Great strength and determination always lie within me.

- My dreams are far more important than my fears. I will keep going no matter what.

- Today, I choose to create magic and miracles in my life.

- My success or failures do not define me. They help me learn and grow.

- I live in perfect alignment with my highest truth.

- I am creating a life that is aligned with my heart and my soul.

- I have the confidence and courage to continue to build my dreams.

- I am focused and persistent and I will never give up.

- Money comes to me easily and effortlessly from all directions.

- I am in charge of my life, and I choose to create my own reality.

- Whatever I put my mind to, I can achieve. I believe in myself, always.

- I am not a product of my circumstances. I am a product of my decisions.

- My energy creates my reality. What I focus on is what I will manifest.

- I am dedicated to living in alignment with my purpose.

- I love the life I am creating and I'm grateful for the opportunities that flow to me with ease.

- I have the courage to walk my own path and to follow my dreams.

- My intuition never lets me down. I always trust it.

- My faith is always bigger than any fears I may have.

- I always follow my heart's path and I am guided by my soul.

- I trust myself and turn inward to seek my highest truth.

- My life works beautifully as I navigate my path with grace and ease.

- I am worthy of making more money in my life and in my business.

- I follow my intuition and know that nothing is put before me that I cannot handle.

- Everything feels so aligned right now; I trust I am on the right path for me.

- Today I face everything with great courage, grace, and strength.

- I see magic and abundance everywhere I look and everywhere I go.

- I am aligned with my truth, and I allow my heart to always guide me.

- I am open to money coming to me from new ways that I've never imagined.

- I always have enough money for everything that I need.

- I handle my success with great love and confidence.

- I am fully supported making money doing what I love.

- I am aligned with the energy of abundance and manifestation.

- I believe in myself and that I have what it takes to succeed.

- It is safe for me to make money. I am worthy of success and prosperity.

- I execute my visions with clarity, focus, and confidence.

- I am always being guided to living my heart's desires.

- The Universe supports my business with an abundance of resources, opportunities, and experiences.

- My energy is authentic and powerful. People from everywhere are drawn to me by my clear and pure vibration.

- I transform my obstacles into opportunities for improvement and growth.

- I am connected to the endless abundance and magic of the Universe.

- I commit to my success, my goals, and my dreams.

- I am a winner and I celebrate all my wins – big and small.

- Every day I align with my highest potential and my unique gifts and natural abilities.

- I lead with integrity, passion, creativity, and care.

- I shift from procrastination to implementing action steps to move me towards my goals.

- Challenges are opportunities for me to learn, grow, improve, and evolve.

- I establish a healthy and harmonious work and life balance.

- I am on the path to spiritual and financial freedom.

- I choose to release limiting beliefs that hinder the success of my inner growth.

- o My life is a creative expression of who I am.

- o I am happy, successful, and fulfilled in my life and in my business.

- o I do what it takes to achieve my next breakthrough.

- o I am grateful for what I already have and for all that I will receive.

- o I am worthy of the finest things that life has to offer.

- o My success encourages others to go after their dreams.

- o I lovingly forgive my past money mistakes and open myself up to receiving more.

- o I love turning my creative ideas into financial abundance.

- o I am proud of everything I have achieved so far. I celebrate my successes.

- o I am open and ready to attract everything I dream of and desire.

- o I use money to better my life and the lives of others.

- o I have the power to attract money and financial wealth.

- o I am worthy of success in all areas of my life.

- o I have everything I need inside of me to achieve my dreams.

- o I can create and manifest the desires of my heart.

- o I am confident, strong, and unstoppable.

- o Money is pouring into my life from all directions.

- o What I choose to focus on grows and so I focus on creating a life I truly desire.

o   My service is a gift to this world, and I feel compelled to share it with others.

o   I am becoming more and more successful every single day. For this I am grateful.

o   My work makes a powerful difference in the world.

o   I believe in the value I create in the lives of others through my business ventures.

o   My income is growing every day by doing something I absolutely love.

o   The passion I have for my work enables me to create real value in the world.

o   My failures have made me a better person. They have contributed to my growth and success.

o   I am driven by my passions, my purpose, and my greatest potential.

o   I attract the right people in my life through my authentic and genuine energy.

o   My dreams and my desires align with my core values and beliefs.

Date: _______________________

Current energy level: ☹ ☹ 😐 ☺ 😄

I am grateful for:

____
____
____
____
____
____
____
____

My empowering affirmation:

____
____
____
____

Three things I will do for self-care:

1. ____________________________________
2. ____________________________________
3. ____________________________________

My intention for today:

____
____
____
____

Three goals for the day:

1. ___________________________
   ____
2. ___________________________
   ____
3. ___________________________
   ____

Evening self-reflection:

____
____
____
____
____
____
____
____
____
____
____
____
____
____
____
____
____
____

Completed:

- [ ] Gratitude
- [ ] Affirmation
- [ ] Self-Care
- [ ] Intention
- [ ] Goals
- [ ] Self-Reflection

Date: _______________

Current energy level: ☹ ☹ 😐 ☺ 😊

I am grateful for:

____
____
____
____
____
____
____

My empowering affirmation:

____
____
____
____

Three things I will do for self-care:

1. _______________________________________
2. _______________________________________
3. _______________________________________

My intention for today:

____
____
____
____

Three goals for the day:

1. ______________________________________
   ____
2. ______________________________________
   ____
3. ______________________________________
   ____

Evening self-reflection:

____
____
____
____
____
____
____
____
____
____
____
____
____
____
____
____
____
____

Completed:

- [ ] Gratitude
- [ ] Affirmation
- [ ] Self-Care
- [ ] Intention
- [ ] Goals
- [ ] Self-Reflection

Date: _______________________

Current energy level: ☹ ☹ ☺ ☺ ☺

I am grateful for:

____
____
____
____
____
____
____
____

My empowering affirmation:

____
____
____
____

Three things I will do for self-care:

1. ___________________________________
2. ___________________________________
3. ___________________________________

My intention for today:

____
____
____
____

Three goals for the day:

1. _______________________________________
   ____
2. _______________________________________
   ____
3. _______________________________________
   ____

Evening self-reflection:

Completed:

- [ ] Gratitude
- [ ] Affirmation
- [ ] Self-Care
- [ ] Intention
- [ ] Goals
- [ ] Self-Reflection

Date: _______________________

Current energy level: ☹ ☹ 😐 🙂 😃

I am grateful for:

____
____
____
____
____
____
____
____

My empowering affirmation:

____
____
____
____

Three things I will do for self-care:

   1. ______________________________________
   2. ______________________________________
   3. ______________________________________

My intention for today:

____
____
____
____

Three goals for the day:

1. ______________________________

   ____

2. ______________________________

   ____

3. ______________________________

   ____

Evening self-reflection:

Completed:

☐ Gratitude   ☐ Intention
☐ Affirmation   ☐ Goals
☐ Self-Care   ☐ Self-Reflection

Date: _______________________

Current energy level: ☹ ☹ 😐 🙂 😃

I am grateful for:

____
____
____
____
____
____
____

My empowering affirmation:

____
____
____
____

Three things I will do for self-care:

1. ____________________________________
2. ____________________________________
3. ____________________________________

My intention for today:

____
____
____
____

Three goals for the day:

1. _______________________________
   ____
2. _______________________________
   ____
3. _______________________________
   ____

Evening self-reflection:

____
____
____
____
____
____
____
____
____
____
____
____
____
____
____
____
____

Completed:

- [ ] Gratitude
- [ ] Affirmation
- [ ] Self-Care
- [ ] Intention
- [ ] Goals
- [ ] Self-Reflection

Date: _______________________

Current energy level: ☹ ☹ ☺ ☺ ☺

I am grateful for:

____
____
____
____
____
____
____
____

My empowering affirmation:

____
____
____
____

Three things I will do for self-care:

1. ____________________________
2. ____________________________
3. ____________________________

My intention for today:

____
____
____

Three goals for the day:

1. ______________________________
   ____
2. ______________________________
   ____
3. ______________________________
   ____

Evening self-reflection:

____
____
____
____
____
____
____
____
____
____
____
____
____
____
____
____
____

Completed:

- ☐ Gratitude
- ☐ Affirmation
- ☐ Self-Care
- ☐ Intention
- ☐ Goals
- ☐ Self-Reflection

Date: _______________________

Current energy level: ☹ ☹ 😐 🙂 😊

I am grateful for:

____
____
____
____
____
____
____
____

My empowering affirmation:

____
____
____
____

Three things I will do for self-care:

1. ____________________________________
2. ____________________________________
3. ____________________________________

My intention for today:

____
____
____
____

Three goals for the day:

1. ____
   ____
2. ____
   ____
3. ____
   ____

Evening self-reflection:

____
____
____
____
____
____
____
____
____
____
____
____
____
____
____
____
____
____

Completed:

- [ ] Gratitude
- [ ] Affirmation
- [ ] Self-Care
- [ ] Intention
- [ ] Goals
- [ ] Self-Reflection

Date: _______________________

Current energy level: ☹ ☹ 😐 🙂 😊

I am grateful for:

____
____
____
____
____
____
____

My empowering affirmation:

____
____
____
____

Three things I will do for self-care:

    1. _______________________________
    2. _______________________________
    3. _______________________________

My intention for today:

____
____
____
____

Three goals for the day:

1. ___________________________
   ____
2. ___________________________
   ____
3. ___________________________
   ____

Evening self-reflection:

____
____
____
____
____
____
____
____
____
____
____
____
____
____
____
____
____

Completed:

☐ Gratitude   ☐ Intention
☐ Affirmation   ☐ Goals
☐ Self-Care   ☐ Self-Reflection

Date: _______________________

Current energy level: 🙁 🙁 😐 🙂 😊

I am grateful for:

____
____
____
____
____
____
____

My empowering affirmation:

____
____
____
____

Three things I will do for self-care:

1. ____________________________________
2. ____________________________________
3. ____________________________________

My intention for today:

____
____
____
____

Three goals for the day:

1. ________________________________
   ____
2. ________________________________
   ____
3. ________________________________
   ____

Evening self-reflection:

____
____
____
____
____
____
____
____
____
____
____
____
____
____
____
____
____
____

Completed:

- ☐ Gratitude
- ☐ Affirmation
- ☐ Self-Care
- ☐ Intention
- ☐ Goals
- ☐ Self-Reflection

Date: _______________________

Current energy level: ☹ ☹ 😐 🙂 😊

I am grateful for:

____
____
____
____
____
____
____
____

My empowering affirmation:

____
____
____
____

Three things I will do for self-care:

1. ____________________________________
2. ____________________________________
3. ____________________________________

My intention for today:

____
____
____
____

Three goals for the day:

1. ______________________________
   ____
2. ______________________________
   ____
3. ______________________________
   ____

Evening self-reflection:

Completed:

- [ ] Gratitude
- [ ] Affirmation
- [ ] Self-Care
- [ ] Intention
- [ ] Goals
- [ ] Self-Reflection

Date: _______________________

Current energy level: ☹ ☹ 😐 🙂 😊

I am grateful for:

____

____

____

____

____

____

____

____

My empowering affirmation:

____

____

____

____

Three things I will do for self-care:

1. _______________________________________
2. _______________________________________
3. _______________________________________

My intention for today:

____

____

____

Three goals for the day:

1. _______________________________

2. _______________________________

3. _______________________________

Evening self-reflection:

Completed:

- [ ] Gratitude
- [ ] Affirmation
- [ ] Self-Care
- [ ] Intention
- [ ] Goals
- [ ] Self-Reflection

Date: _______________________

Current energy level: ☹ ☹ 😐 🙂 😊

I am grateful for:

____
____
____
____
____
____
____
____

My empowering affirmation:

____
____
____
____

Three things I will do for self-care:

    1. _______________________________________
    2. _______________________________________
    3. _______________________________________

My intention for today:

____
____
____
____

Three goals for the day:

1. ___________________________________
   ____
2. ___________________________________
   ____
3. ___________________________________
   ____

Evening self-reflection:

____
____
____
____
____
____
____
____
____
____
____
____
____
____
____
____
____
____

Completed:

- [ ] Gratitude
- [ ] Affirmation
- [ ] Self-Care
- [ ] Intention
- [ ] Goals
- [ ] Self-Reflection

Date: _______________________

Current energy level: ☹ ☹ 😐 🙂 😊

I am grateful for:

____
____
____
____
____
____
____
____

My empowering affirmation:

____
____
____
____

Three things I will do for self-care:

1. ______________________________________
2. ______________________________________
3. ______________________________________

My intention for today:

____
____
____
____

Three goals for the day:

1. _______________________________

____

2. _______________________________

____

3. _______________________________

____

Evening self-reflection:

Completed:

- ☐ Gratitude
- ☐ Affirmation
- ☐ Self-Care
- ☐ Intention
- ☐ Goals
- ☐ Self-Reflection

Date: _______________________

Current energy level: ☹ ☹ 😐 🙂 😊

I am grateful for:

____
____
____
____
____
____
____

My empowering affirmation:

____
____
____
____

Three things I will do for self-care:

1. ___________________________________
2. ___________________________________
3. ___________________________________

My intention for today:

____
____
____
____

Three goals for the day:

1. ____

____

2. ____

____

3. ____

____

Evening self-reflection:

Completed:

☐ Gratitude   ☐ Intention

☐ Affirmation   ☐ Goals

☐ Self-Care   ☐ Self-Reflection

Date: _______________________

Current energy level: ☹ ☹ ☺ ☺ ☺

I am grateful for:

____
____
____
____
____
____
____
____

My empowering affirmation:

____
____
____
____

Three things I will do for self-care:

1. _________________________________
2. _________________________________
3. _________________________________

My intention for today:

____
____
____
____

Three goals for the day:

    1. _______________________________

    2. _______________________________

    3. _______________________________

Evening self-reflection:

Completed:

- ☐ Gratitude
- ☐ Affirmation
- ☐ Self-Care
- ☐ Intention
- ☐ Goals
- ☐ Self-Reflection

Date: _______________________

Current energy level: ☹ ☹ 😐 🙂 😊

I am grateful for:

____
____
____
____
____
____
____

My empowering affirmation:

____
____
____
____

Three things I will do for self-care:

1. ____________________________________
2. ____________________________________
3. ____________________________________

My intention for today:

____
____
____
____

Three goals for the day:

1. _______________________________________

2. _______________________________________

3. _______________________________________

Evening self-reflection:

____
____
____
____
____
____
____
____
____
____
____
____
____
____
____
____
____
____
____
____

Completed:

☐ Gratitude   ☐ Intention
☐ Affirmation   ☐ Goals
☐ Self-Care   ☐ Self-Reflection

Date: ________________

Current energy level: ☹ ☹ 😐 ☺ ☺

I am grateful for:

____
____
____
____
____
____
____
____

My empowering affirmation:

____
____
____
____

Three things I will do for self-care:

1. ____________________________
2. ____________________________
3. ____________________________

My intention for today:

____
____
____
____

Three goals for the day:

1. _______________________________

____

2. _______________________________

____

3. _______________________________

____

Evening self-reflection:

Completed:

- ☐ Gratitude
- ☐ Affirmation
- ☐ Self-Care
- ☐ Intention
- ☐ Goals
- ☐ Self-Reflection

Date: _______________________

Current energy level: ☹ ☹ ☺ ☺ ☺

I am grateful for:

____
____
____
____
____
____
____
____

My empowering affirmation:

____
____
____
____

Three things I will do for self-care:

1. _______________________________
2. _______________________________
3. _______________________________

My intention for today:

____
____
____
____

Three goals for the day:

1. _______________________________

2. _______________________________

3. _______________________________

Evening self-reflection:

Completed:

- [ ] Gratitude
- [ ] Affirmation
- [ ] Self-Care
- [ ] Intention
- [ ] Goals
- [ ] Self-Reflection

Date: _______________________

Current energy level: ☹ ☹ 😐 🙂 😊

I am grateful for:

____
____
____
____
____
____
____
____

My empowering affirmation:

____
____
____
____

Three things I will do for self-care:

1. _____________________________________
2. _____________________________________
3. _____________________________________

My intention for today:

____
____
____
____

Three goals for the day:

1. ______________________________________
   ____
2. ______________________________________
   ____
3. ______________________________________
   ____

Evening self-reflection:

____
____
____
____
____
____
____
____
____
____
____
____
____
____
____
____
____
____

Completed:

- [ ] Gratitude
- [ ] Affirmation
- [ ] Self-Care
- [ ] Intention
- [ ] Goals
- [ ] Self-Reflection

Date: _______________________

Current energy level: ☹ ☹ 😐 🙂 😊

I am grateful for:

____
____
____
____
____
____
____
____

My empowering affirmation:

____
____
____
____

Three things I will do for self-care:

1. ____________________________________
2. ____________________________________
3. ____________________________________

My intention for today:

____
____
____

Three goals for the day:

1. ______________________________
   ____
2. ______________________________
   ____
3. ______________________________
   ____

Evening self-reflection:

____
____
____
____
____
____
____
____
____
____
____
____
____
____
____
____
____

Completed:

- [ ] Gratitude
- [ ] Affirmation
- [ ] Self-Care
- [ ] Intention
- [ ] Goals
- [ ] Self-Reflection

Date: _______________________

Current energy level: ☹ ☹ 😐 ☺ 😃

I am grateful for:

____
____
____
____
____
____
____

My empowering affirmation:

____
____
____
____

Three things I will do for self-care:

1. ____________________________________
2. ____________________________________
3. ____________________________________

My intention for today:

____
____
____

Three goals for the day:

1. _______________________________

2. _______________________________

3. _______________________________

Evening self-reflection:

Completed:

- [ ] Gratitude
- [ ] Affirmation
- [ ] Self-Care
- [ ] Intention
- [ ] Goals
- [ ] Self-Reflection

Date: ___________________________

Current energy level: ☹ ☹ 😐 🙂 😊

I am grateful for:

____
____
____
____
____
____
____
____

My empowering affirmation:

____
____
____
____

Three things I will do for self-care:

1. ____________________________________
2. ____________________________________
3. ____________________________________

My intention for today:

____
____
____
____

Three goals for the day:

1. _______________________________

2. _______________________________

3. _______________________________

Evening self-reflection:

Completed:

- ☐ Gratitude
- ☐ Affirmation
- ☐ Self-Care
- ☐ Intention
- ☐ Goals
- ☐ Self-Reflection

Date: _______________________

Current energy level: ☹ ☹ ☺ ☺ ☺

I am grateful for:

____
____
____
____
____
____
____

My empowering affirmation:

____
____
____
____

Three things I will do for self-care:

1. ____________________________________
2. ____________________________________
3. ____________________________________

My intention for today:

____
____
____
____

Three goals for the day:

1. ____

2. ____

3. ____

Evening self-reflection:

Completed:

- [ ] Gratitude
- [ ] Affirmation
- [ ] Self-Care
- [ ] Intention
- [ ] Goals
- [ ] Self-Reflection

Date: _______________________

Current energy level: ☹ ☹ ☺ ☺ ☺

I am grateful for:

____
____
____
____
____
____
____
____

My empowering affirmation:

____
____
____
____

Three things I will do for self-care:

1. ____________________________________
2. ____________________________________
3. ____________________________________

My intention for today:

____
____
____

Three goals for the day:

1. ______________________________
   ____
2. ______________________________
   ____
3. ______________________________
   ____

Evening self-reflection:

Completed:

- ☐ Gratitude
- ☐ Affirmation
- ☐ Self-Care
- ☐ Intention
- ☐ Goals
- ☐ Self-Reflection

Date: _______________________

Current energy level: ☹ ☹ 😐 🙂 😊

I am grateful for:

____
____
____
____
____
____
____
____

My empowering affirmation:

____
____
____
____

Three things I will do for self-care:

1. _______________________
2. _______________________
3. _______________________

My intention for today:

____
____
____

Three goals for the day:

1. _______________________________
____
2. _______________________________
____
3. _______________________________
____

Evening self-reflection:

____
____
____
____
____
____
____
____
____
____
____
____
____
____
____
____
____

Completed:

☐ Gratitude   ☐ Intention
☐ Affirmation   ☐ Goals
☐ Self-Care   ☐ Self-Reflection

Date: _______________________

Current energy level: ☹ ☹ ☺ ☺ ☺

I am grateful for:

____
____
____
____
____
____
____
____

My empowering affirmation:

____
____
____
____

Three things I will do for self-care:

1. _______________________________
2. _______________________________
3. _______________________________

My intention for today:

____
____
____
____

Three goals for the day:

1. _______________________________________

   ____

2. _______________________________________

   ____

3. _______________________________________

   ____

Evening self-reflection:

____

____

____

____

____

____

____

____

____

____

____

____

____

____

____

____

____

____

Completed:

- ☐ Gratitude
- ☐ Affirmation
- ☐ Self-Care
- ☐ Intention
- ☐ Goals
- ☐ Self-Reflection

Date: _______________________

Current energy level: ☹ ☹ ☺ ☺ ☺

I am grateful for:

____
____
____
____
____
____
____
____

My empowering affirmation:

____
____
____

Three things I will do for self-care:

1. ____________________________________
2. ____________________________________
3. ____________________________________

My intention for today:

____
____
____

Three goals for the day:

1. _______________________________________

2. _______________________________________

3. _______________________________________

Evening self-reflection:

Completed:

- [ ] Gratitude
- [ ] Affirmation
- [ ] Self-Care
- [ ] Intention
- [ ] Goals
- [ ] Self-Reflection

Date: _______________________

Current energy level: ☹ ☹ 😐 🙂 😃

I am grateful for:

____

____

____

____

____

____

____

My empowering affirmation:

____

____

____

____

Three things I will do for self-care:

1. _______________________________________

2. _______________________________________

3. _______________________________________

My intention for today:

____

____

____

____

Three goals for the day:

1. ____
   ____
2. ____
   ____
3. ____
   ____

Evening self-reflection:

____
____
____
____
____
____
____
____
____
____
____
____
____
____
____
____
____
____

Completed:

- ☐ Gratitude
- ☐ Affirmation
- ☐ Self-Care
- ☐ Intention
- ☐ Goals
- ☐ Self-Reflection

Date: _______________

Current energy level: ☹ ☹ 😐 🙂 😊

I am grateful for:

____
____
____
____
____
____
____
____

My empowering affirmation:

____
____
____
____

Three things I will do for self-care:

1. _____________________________
2. _____________________________
3. _____________________________

My intention for today:

____
____
____
____

Three goals for the day:

1. ______________________________________

2. ______________________________________

3. ______________________________________

Evening self-reflection:

Completed:

☐ Gratitude   ☐ Intention
☐ Affirmation   ☐ Goals
☐ Self-Care   ☐ Self-Reflection

Date: _______________________

Current energy level: ☹ ☹ ☺ ☺ ☺

I am grateful for:

____
____
____
____
____
____
____
____

My empowering affirmation:

____
____
____
____

Three things I will do for self-care:

    1. ____________________________
    2. ____________________________
    3. ____________________________

My intention for today:

____
____
____
____

Three goals for the day:

1. _______________________________
   ____
2. _______________________________
   ____
3. _______________________________
   ____

Evening self-reflection:

Completed:

- ☐ Gratitude
- ☐ Affirmation
- ☐ Self-Care
- ☐ Intention
- ☐ Goals
- ☐ Self-Reflection

Date: _______________________

Current energy level: ☹ ☹ 😐 🙂 😊

I am grateful for:

____
____
____
____
____
____
____
____

My empowering affirmation:

____
____
____
____

Three things I will do for self-care:

1. ___________________________________
2. ___________________________________
3. ___________________________________

My intention for today:

____
____
____
____

Three goals for the day:

1. _______________________________
   ____
2. _______________________________
   ____
3. _______________________________
   ____

Evening self-reflection:

Completed:

- [ ] Gratitude
- [ ] Affirmation
- [ ] Self-Care
- [ ] Intention
- [ ] Goals
- [ ] Self-Reflection

Date: _______________________

Current energy level: ☹ ☹ ☺ ☺ ☺

I am grateful for:

____
____
____
____
____
____
____

My empowering affirmation:

____
____
____
____

Three things I will do for self-care:

1. ____________________________________
2. ____________________________________
3. ____________________________________

My intention for today:

____
____
____
____

Three goals for the day:

1. ____

____

2. ____

____

3. ____

____

Evening self-reflection:

\
____

____

____

____

____

____

____

____

____

____

____

____

____

____

____

____

____

____

____

Completed:

☐ Gratitude   ☐ Intention
☐ Affirmation   ☐ Goals
☐ Self-Care   ☐ Self-Reflection

Date: _______________________

Current energy level: ☹ ☹ 😐 ☺ 😄

I am grateful for:

____
____
____
____
____
____
____
____
____

My empowering affirmation:

____
____
____
____

Three things I will do for self-care:

1. _____________________________________
2. _____________________________________
3. _____________________________________

My intention for today:

____
____
____
____

Three goals for the day:

1. _______________________________

2. _______________________________

3. _______________________________

....

Evening self-reflection:

____

____

____

____

____

____

____

____

____

____

____

____

____

____

____

Completed:

- [ ] Gratitude
- [ ] Affirmation
- [ ] Self-Care
- [ ] Intention
- [ ] Goals
- [ ] Self-Reflection

Date: _______________________

Current energy level: ☹ ☹ 😐 🙂 😊

I am grateful for:

____
____
____
____
____
____
____
____

My empowering affirmation:

____
____
____
____

Three things I will do for self-care:

1. ___________________________________
2. ___________________________________
3. ___________________________________

My intention for today:

____
____
____
____

Three goals for the day:

1. _______________________________________

2. _______________________________________

3. _______________________________________

Evening self-reflection:

Completed:

- [ ] Gratitude
- [ ] Affirmation
- [ ] Self-Care
- [ ] Intention
- [ ] Goals
- [ ] Self-Reflection

Date: _______________________

Current energy level: ☹ ☹ 😐 ☺ 😊

I am grateful for:

____
____
____
____
____
____
____
____

My empowering affirmation:

____
____
____
____

Three things I will do for self-care:

1. ______________________________________
2. ______________________________________
3. ______________________________________

My intention for today:

____
____
____
____

Three goals for the day:

1. ____
____
2. ____
____
3. ____
____

Evening self-reflection:

____
____
____
____
____
____
____
____
____
____
____
____
____
____
____
____
____
____
____

Completed:

☐ Gratitude   ☐ Intention
☐ Affirmation   ☐ Goals
☐ Self-Care   ☐ Self-Reflection

Date: ______________________

Current energy level: ☹ ☹ ☺ ☺ ☺

I am grateful for:

____
____
____
____
____
____
____
____

My empowering affirmation:

____
____
____
____

Three things I will do for self-care:

1. ____________________________________
2. ____________________________________
3. ____________________________________

My intention for today:

____
____
____

Three goals for the day:

1. ____
   ____
2. ____
   ____
3. ____
   ____

Evening self-reflection:

____
____
____
____
____
____
____
____
____
____
____
____
____
____
____
____
____
____
____

Completed:

- [ ] Gratitude
- [ ] Affirmation
- [ ] Self-Care
- [ ] Intention
- [ ] Goals
- [ ] Self-Reflection

Date: _______________________

Current energy level: ☹ ☹ 😐 🙂 😃

I am grateful for:

____

____

____

____

____

____

____

____

My empowering affirmation:

____

____

____

____

Three things I will do for self-care:

1. ___________________________________

2. ___________________________________

3. ___________________________________

My intention for today:

____

____

____

____

Three goals for the day:

1. ______________________________
   ____
2. ______________________________
   ____
3. ______________________________
   ____

Evening self-reflection:

Completed:

- [ ] Gratitude
- [ ] Affirmation
- [ ] Self-Care
- [ ] Intention
- [ ] Goals
- [ ] Self-Reflection

Date: _______________

Current energy level: ☹ ☹ ☺ ☺ ☺

I am grateful for:

____
____
____
____
____
____
____
____

My empowering affirmation:

____
____
____
____

Three things I will do for self-care:

1. _______________
2. _______________
3. _______________

My intention for today:

____
____
____
____

Three goals for the day:

1. _______________________________
   ____
2. _______________________________
   ____
3. _______________________________
   ____

Evening self-reflection:

Completed:

- ☐ Gratitude
- ☐ Affirmation
- ☐ Self-Care
- ☐ Intention
- ☐ Goals
- ☐ Self-Reflection

Date: _______________________

Current energy level: ☹ ☹ 😐 ☺ 😃

I am grateful for:

____
____
____
____
____
____
____
____

My empowering affirmation:

____
____
____
____

Three things I will do for self-care:

1. ____________________________________
2. ____________________________________
3. ____________________________________

My intention for today:

____
____
____
____

Three goals for the day:

1. ______________________________
   ____
2. ______________________________
   ____
3. ______________________________
   ____

Evening self-reflection:

____
____
____
____
____
____
____
____
____
____
____
____
____
____
____
____
____
____

Completed:

- ☐ Gratitude
- ☐ Affirmation
- ☐ Self-Care
- ☐ Intention
- ☐ Goals
- ☐ Self-Reflection

Date: _______________________

Current energy level: ☹ ☹ ☺ ☺ ☺

I am grateful for:

____
____
____
____
____
____
____
____

My empowering affirmation:

____
____
____
____

Three things I will do for self-care:

1. ___________________________________
2. ___________________________________
3. ___________________________________

My intention for today:

____
____
____
____

Three goals for the day:

1. ____

____

2. ____

____

3. ____

____

Evening self-reflection:

____
____
____
____
____
____
____
____
____
____
____
____
____
____
____
____
____
____

Completed:

- ☐ Gratitude
- ☐ Affirmation
- ☐ Self-Care
- ☐ Intention
- ☐ Goals
- ☐ Self-Reflection

Date: _______________________

Current energy level: ☹ ☹ 😐 🙂 😃

I am grateful for:

____
____
____
____
____
____
____
____

My empowering affirmation:

____
____
____
____

Three things I will do for self-care:

1. ____________________________________
2. ____________________________________
3. ____________________________________

My intention for today:

____
____
____
____

Three goals for the day:

1. ____

2. ____

3. ____

Evening self-reflection:

Completed:

- [ ] Gratitude
- [ ] Affirmation
- [ ] Self-Care
- [ ] Intention
- [ ] Goals
- [ ] Self-Reflection

Date: _______________________

Current energy level: ☹ ☹ 😐 🙂 😊

I am grateful for:

____
____
____
____
____
____
____

My empowering affirmation:

____
____
____
____

Three things I will do for self-care:

1. ____________________________________
2. ____________________________________
3. ____________________________________

My intention for today:

____
____
____
____

Three goals for the day:

1. ____

   ____

2. ____

   ____

3. ____

   ____

Evening self-reflection:

____

____

____

____

____

____

____

____

____

____

____

____

____

____

____

____

____

____

____

Completed:

☐ Gratitude   ☐ Intention
☐ Affirmation   ☐ Goals
☐ Self-Care   ☐ Self-Reflection

Date: _______________________

Current energy level: ☹ ☹ 😐 🙂 😊

I am grateful for:

____
____
____
____
____
____
____
____

My empowering affirmation:

____
____
____
____

Three things I will do for self-care:

    1. _______________________________
    2. _______________________________
    3. _______________________________

My intention for today:

____
____
____
____

Three goals for the day:

1. _______________________________

2. _______________________________

3. _______________________________

. . . .

Evening self-reflection:

____

____

____

____

____

____

____

____

____

____

____

____

____

____

____

____

____

Completed:

- ☐ Gratitude
- ☐ Affirmation
- ☐ Self-Care
- ☐ Intention
- ☐ Goals
- ☐ Self-Reflection

Date: _______________________

Current energy level: ☹ ☹ 😐 ☺ 😊

I am grateful for:

____
____
____
____
____
____
____

My empowering affirmation:

____
____
____
____

Three things I will do for self-care:

1. ___________________________________
2. ___________________________________
3. ___________________________________

My intention for today:

____
____
____

Three goals for the day:

1. _______________________________
____
2. _______________________________
____
3. _______________________________
____

Evening self-reflection:

Completed:

- [ ] Gratitude
- [ ] Affirmation
- [ ] Self-Care
- [ ] Intention
- [ ] Goals
- [ ] Self-Reflection

Date: ___________________________

Current energy level: ☹ ☹ 😐 🙂 😊

I am grateful for:

____
____
____
____
____
____
____
____

My empowering affirmation:

____
____
____
____

Three things I will do for self-care:

1. ____________________________________
2. ____________________________________
3. ____________________________________

My intention for today:

____
____
____
____

Three goals for the day:

1. _______________________________________
   ____
2. _______________________________________
   ____
3. _______________________________________
   ____

Evening self-reflection:

____
____
____
____
____
____
____
____
____
____
____
____
____
____
____
____
____
____

Completed:

☐ Gratitude   ☐ Intention
☐ Affirmation   ☐ Goals
☐ Self-Care   ☐ Self-Reflection

Date: _______________________

Current energy level: ☹ ☹ 😐 🙂 😊

I am grateful for:

____
____
____
____
____
____
____
____

My empowering affirmation:

____
____
____
____

Three things I will do for self-care:

1. ____
2. ____
3. ____

My intention for today:

____
____
____
____

Three goals for the day:

1. _______________________________
   ____
2. _______________________________
   ____
3. _______________________________
   ____

Evening self-reflection:

Completed:

- [ ] Gratitude
- [ ] Affirmation
- [ ] Self-Care
- [ ] Intention
- [ ] Goals
- [ ] Self-Reflection

Date: ________________________

Current energy level: ☹ ☹ 😐 🙂 😊

I am grateful for:

____
____
____
____
____
____
____
____

My empowering affirmation:

____
____
____
____

Three things I will do for self-care:

1. ___________________________________
2. ___________________________________
3. ___________________________________

My intention for today:

____
____
____
____

Three goals for the day:

1. _______________________________
   ____
2. _______________________________
   ____
3. _______________________________
   ____

Evening self-reflection:

Completed:

☐ Gratitude   ☐ Intention
☐ Affirmation   ☐ Goals
☐ Self-Care   ☐ Self-Reflection

Date: _______________________

Current energy level: ☹ ☹ 😐 🙂 😊

I am grateful for:

____
____
____
____
____
____
____
____

My empowering affirmation:

____
____
____
____

Three things I will do for self-care:

1. ____
2. ____
3. ____

My intention for today:

____
____
____
____

Three goals for the day:

1. ________________________________
   ____
2. ________________________________
   ____
3. ________________________________
   ____

Evening self-reflection:

____
____
____
____
____
____
____
____
____
____
____
____
____
____
____
____
____
____

Completed:

- ☐ Gratitude
- ☐ Affirmation
- ☐ Self-Care
- ☐ Intention
- ☐ Goals
- ☐ Self-Reflection

Date: _______________________

Current energy level: ☹ ☹ 😐 🙂 😊

I am grateful for:

____
____
____
____
____
____
____
____

My empowering affirmation:

____
____
____
____

Three things I will do for self-care:

1. ____________________________________
2. ____________________________________
3. ____________________________________

My intention for today:

____
____
____
____

Three goals for the day:

1. ___________________________________
   ____
2. ___________________________________
   ____
3. ___________________________________
   ____

Evening self-reflection:

____
____
____
____
____
____
____
____
____
____
____
____
____
____
____
____
____
____
____

Completed:

☐ Gratitude   ☐ Intention
☐ Affirmation   ☐ Goals
☐ Self-Care   ☐ Self-Reflection

Date: _______________________

Current energy level: ☹ ☹ 😐 🙂 😊

I am grateful for:

____
____
____
____
____
____
____

My empowering affirmation:

____
____
____
____

Three things I will do for self-care:

1. ___________________________________
2. ___________________________________
3. ___________________________________

My intention for today:

____
____
____
____

Three goals for the day:

1. _______________________________

2. _______________________________

3. _______________________________

Evening self-reflection:

Completed:

- ☐ Gratitude
- ☐ Affirmation
- ☐ Self-Care
- ☐ Intention
- ☐ Goals
- ☐ Self-Reflection

Date: _______________________

Current energy level: ☹ ☹ 😐 🙂 😊

I am grateful for:

____
____
____
____
____
____
____

My empowering affirmation:

____
____
____
____

Three things I will do for self-care:

1. ___________________________________
2. ___________________________________
3. ___________________________________

My intention for today:

____
____
____
____

Three goals for the day:

1. _______________________________

2. _______________________________

3. _______________________________

....

Evening self-reflection:

____
____
____
____
____
____
____
____
____
____
____
____
____
____
____
____
____
____

Completed:

☐ Gratitude   ☐ Intention
☐ Affirmation   ☐ Goals
☐ Self-Care   ☐ Self-Reflection

Date: _______________________

Current energy level: ☹ ☹ 😐 🙂 😃

I am grateful for:

____
____
____
____
____
____
____
____

My empowering affirmation:

____
____
____
____

Three things I will do for self-care:

1. ________________________________
2. ________________________________
3. ________________________________

My intention for today:

____
____
____
____

Three goals for the day:

1. ___________________________________

____

2. ___________________________________

____

3. ___________________________________

____

Evening self-reflection:

____

____

____

____

____

____

____

____

____

____

____

____

____

____

____

____

____

____

Completed:

- ☐ Gratitude
- ☐ Affirmation
- ☐ Self-Care
- ☐ Intention
- ☐ Goals
- ☐ Self-Reflection

Date: _______________________

Current energy level: ☹ ☹ 😐 🙂 😊

I am grateful for:

____

____

____

____

____

____

____

____

My empowering affirmation:

____

____

____

____

Three things I will do for self-care:

1. _________________________________

2. _________________________________

3. _________________________________

My intention for today:

____

____

____

____

Three goals for the day:

1. _______________________________
____
2. _______________________________
____
3. _______________________________
____

Evening self-reflection:

____
____
____
____
____
____
____
____
____
____
____
____
____
____
____
____
____
____

Completed:

- ☐ Gratitude
- ☐ Affirmation
- ☐ Self-Care
- ☐ Intention
- ☐ Goals
- ☐ Self-Reflection

Date: _______________________

Current energy level: ☹ ☹ 😐 🙂 😊

I am grateful for:

____
____
____
____
____
____
____

My empowering affirmation:

____
____
____
____

Three things I will do for self-care:

1. ____
2. ____
3. ____

My intention for today:

____
____
____

Three goals for the day:

1. ____
   ____
2. ____
   ____
3. ____
   ____

Evening self-reflection:

____
____
____
____
____
____
____
____
____
____
____
____
____
____
____
____
____
____

Completed:

- [ ] Gratitude
- [ ] Affirmation
- [ ] Self-Care
- [ ] Intention
- [ ] Goals
- [ ] Self-Reflection

Date: ______________________

Current energy level: ☹ ☹ 😐 🙂 😊

I am grateful for:

____
____
____
____
____
____
____
____

My empowering affirmation:

____
____
____
____

Three things I will do for self-care:

1. ______________________________________
2. ______________________________________
3. ______________________________________

My intention for today:

____
____
____
____

Three goals for the day:

1. _______________________________________
   ____
2. _______________________________________
   ____
3. _______________________________________
   ____

Evening self-reflection:

____
____
____
____
____
____
____
____
____
____
____
____
____
____
____
____
____
____

Completed:

☐ Gratitude   ☐ Intention
☐ Affirmation   ☐ Goals
☐ Self-Care   ☐ Self-Reflection

Date: _______________________

Current energy level: 🙁 ☹ 😐 🙂 😊

I am grateful for:

____
____
____
____
____
____
____
____

My empowering affirmation:

____
____
____
____

Three things I will do for self-care:

1. _____________________________
2. _____________________________
3. _____________________________

My intention for today:

____
____
____
____

Three goals for the day:

   1. _______________________________

       ____

   2. _______________________________

       ____

   3. _______________________________

       ____

Evening self-reflection:

Completed:

- ☐ Gratitude
- ☐ Affirmation
- ☐ Self-Care
- ☐ Intention
- ☐ Goals
- ☐ Self-Reflection

Date: _______________________

Current energy level: ☹ ☹ 😐 🙂 😊

I am grateful for:

____
____
____
____
____
____
____
____

My empowering affirmation:

____
____
____
____

Three things I will do for self-care:

1. ____________________________________
2. ____________________________________
3. ____________________________________

My intention for today:

____
____
____
____

Three goals for the day:

1. ______________________________
____
2. ______________________________
____
3. ______________________________
____

Evening self-reflection:

Completed:

☐ Gratitude   ☐ Intention
☐ Affirmation   ☐ Goals
☐ Self-Care   ☐ Self-Reflection

Date: _______________________

Current energy level: ☹ ☹ 😐 🙂 😊

I am grateful for:

____
____
____
____
____
____
____
____

My empowering affirmation:

____
____
____
____

Three things I will do for self-care:

1. ____________________________________
2. ____________________________________
3. ____________________________________

My intention for today:

____
____
____
____

Three goals for the day:

1. _______________________________

2. _______________________________

3. _______________________________

....

Evening self-reflection:

____

____

____

____

____

____

____

____

____

____

____

____

____

____

____

____

____

____

Completed:

- ☐ Gratitude
- ☐ Affirmation
- ☐ Self-Care
- ☐ Intention
- ☐ Goals
- ☐ Self-Reflection

Date: _______________________

Current energy level: ☹ ☹ 😐 🙂 😊

I am grateful for:

____
____
____
____
____
____
____
____

My empowering affirmation:

____
____
____
____

Three things I will do for self-care:

1. ____
2. ____
3. ____

My intention for today:

____
____
____
____

Three goals for the day:

1. ____
   ____
2. ____
   ____
3. ____
   ____

Evening self-reflection:

Completed:

☐ Gratitude   ☐ Intention
☐ Affirmation   ☐ Goals
☐ Self-Care   ☐ Self-Reflection

Date: ___________________________

Current energy level: ☹ ☹ 😐 🙂 😊

I am grateful for:

____
____
____
____
____
____
____
____

My empowering affirmation:

____
____
____
____

Three things I will do for self-care:

1. ____
2. ____
3. ____

My intention for today:

____
____
____
____

Three goals for the day:

1. _______________________________
____
2. _______________________________
____
3. _______________________________
____

Evening self-reflection:

Completed:

☐ Gratitude
☐ Affirmation
☐ Self-Care

☐ Intention
☐ Goals
☐ Self-Reflection

Date: _______________________

Current energy level: ☹ ☹ 😐 🙂 😊

I am grateful for:

____
____
____
____
____
____
____
____

My empowering affirmation:

____
____
____
____

Three things I will do for self-care:

1. ___________________________
2. ___________________________
3. ___________________________

My intention for today:

____
____
____
____

Three goals for the day:

1. _______________________

2. _______________________

3. _______________________

....

Evening self-reflection:

____

Completed:

- [ ] Gratitude
- [ ] Affirmation
- [ ] Self-Care
- [ ] Intention
- [ ] Goals
- [ ] Self-Reflection

Date: ______________________

Current energy level: ☹ ☹ 😐 🙂 😊

I am grateful for:

____
____
____
____
____
____
____
____

My empowering affirmation:

____
____
____
____

Three things I will do for self-care:

1. ______________________________________
2. ______________________________________
3. ______________________________________

My intention for today:

____
____
____
____

Three goals for the day:

1. _______________________
____
2. _______________________
____
3. _______________________
____

Evening self-reflection:

Completed:

- ☐ Gratitude
- ☐ Affirmation
- ☐ Self-Care
- ☐ Intention
- ☐ Goals
- ☐ Self-Reflection

Date: _______________________

Current energy level: ☹ ☹ 😐 🙂 😊

I am grateful for:

____
____
____
____
____
____
____

My empowering affirmation:

____
____
____
____

Three things I will do for self-care:

1. ____________________________________
2. ____________________________________
3. ____________________________________

My intention for today:

____
____
____
____

Three goals for the day:

1. ________________________________
   ____
2. ________________________________
   ____
3. ________________________________
   ____

Evening self-reflection:

____
____
____
____
____
____
____
____
____
____
____
____
____
____
____
____
____
____
____

Completed:

- ☐ Gratitude
- ☐ Affirmation
- ☐ Self-Care
- ☐ Intention
- ☐ Goals
- ☐ Self-Reflection

Date: ___________________

Current energy level: ☹ ☹ 😐 🙂 😊

I am grateful for:

____
____
____
____
____
____
____
____

My empowering affirmation:

____
____
____
____

Three things I will do for self-care:

1. ____________________________________
2. ____________________________________
3. ____________________________________

My intention for today:

____
____
____
____

Three goals for the day:

1. _______________________________________

   ____

2. _______________________________________

   ____

3. _______________________________________

   ____

Evening self-reflection:

____

____

____

____

____

____

____

____

____

____

____

____

____

____

____

____

____

Completed:

- [ ] Gratitude
- [ ] Affirmation
- [ ] Self-Care
- [ ] Intention
- [ ] Goals
- [ ] Self-Reflection

Date: _______________________

Current energy level: ☹ ☹ 😐 🙂 😊

I am grateful for:

____
____
____
____
____
____
____
____

My empowering affirmation:

____
____
____
____

Three things I will do for self-care:

1. ____________________________________
2. ____________________________________
3. ____________________________________

My intention for today:

____
____
____
____

Three goals for the day:

1. ______________________________

2. ______________________________

3. ______________________________

Evening self-reflection:

____

____

____

____

____

____

____

____

____

____

____

____

____

____

____

____

____

Completed:

☐ Gratitude   ☐ Intention

☐ Affirmation   ☐ Goals

☐ Self-Care   ☐ Self-Reflection

Date: _______________________

Current energy level: ☹ ☹ 😐 ☺ 😊

I am grateful for:

____
____
____
____
____
____
____

My empowering affirmation:

____
____
____
____

Three things I will do for self-care:

1. ____________________________________
2. ____________________________________
3. ____________________________________

My intention for today:

____
____
____
____

Three goals for the day:

1. __________________________
____
2. __________________________
____
3. __________________________
____

Evening self-reflection:

____
____
____
____
____
____
____
____
____
____
____
____
____
____
____
____
____
____

Completed:

- [ ] Gratitude
- [ ] Affirmation
- [ ] Self-Care
- [ ] Intention
- [ ] Goals
- [ ] Self-Reflection

Date: _______________________

Current energy level: ☹ ☹ 😐 🙂 😊

I am grateful for:

____
____
____
____
____
____
____
____

My empowering affirmation:

____
____
____
____

Three things I will do for self-care:

1. ______________________________________
2. ______________________________________
3. ______________________________________

My intention for today:

____
____
____
____

Three goals for the day:

1. _______________________________
____
2. _______________________________
____
3. _______________________________
____

Evening self-reflection:

____
____
____
____
____
____
____
____
____
____
____
____
____
____
____
____
____
____

Completed:

- [ ] Gratitude
- [ ] Affirmation
- [ ] Self-Care
- [ ] Intention
- [ ] Goals
- [ ] Self-Reflection

Date: ______________________

Current energy level: ☹ ☹ 😐 🙂 😊

I am grateful for:

____
____
____
____
____
____
____

My empowering affirmation:

____
____
____
____

Three things I will do for self-care:

1. ______________________________
2. ______________________________
3. ______________________________

My intention for today:

____
____
____

Three goals for the day:

1. _______________________________
____
2. _______________________________
____
3. _______________________________
____

Evening self-reflection:

Completed:

- [ ] Gratitude
- [ ] Affirmation
- [ ] Self-Care
- [ ] Intention
- [ ] Goals
- [ ] Self-Reflection

Date: _______________________

Current energy level: ☹ ☹ 😐 🙂 😊

I am grateful for:

____
____
____
____
____
____
____

My empowering affirmation:

____
____
____
____

Three things I will do for self-care:

1. ____________________________________
2. ____________________________________
3. ____________________________________

My intention for today:

____
____
____
____

Three goals for the day:

1. _______________________________

2. _______________________________

3. _______________________________

Evening self-reflection:

Completed:

- ☐ Gratitude
- ☐ Affirmation
- ☐ Self-Care
- ☐ Intention
- ☐ Goals
- ☐ Self-Reflection

Date: ___________________________

Current energy level: ☹ ☹ 😐 🙂 😊

I am grateful for:

____
____
____
____
____
____
____
____

My empowering affirmation:

____
____
____
____

Three things I will do for self-care:

1. _______________________________________
2. _______________________________________
3. _______________________________________

My intention for today:

____
____
____

Three goals for the day:

1. _______________________________
2. _______________________________
3. _______________________________

Evening self-reflection:

Completed:

- [ ] Gratitude
- [ ] Affirmation
- [ ] Self-Care
- [ ] Intention
- [ ] Goals
- [ ] Self-Reflection

Date: _______________________

Current energy level: ☹ ☹ 😐 🙂 😊

I am grateful for:

____
____
____
____
____
____
____
____

My empowering affirmation:

____
____
____
____

Three things I will do for self-care:

1. ____________________________________
2. ____________________________________
3. ____________________________________

My intention for today:

____
____
____
____

Three goals for the day:

1. ___________________________
   ____
2. ___________________________
   ____
3. ___________________________
   ____

Evening self-reflection:

____
____
____
____
____
____
____
____
____
____
____
____
____
____
____
____
____
____

Completed:

- ☐ Gratitude
- ☐ Affirmation
- ☐ Self-Care
- ☐ Intention
- ☐ Goals
- ☐ Self-Reflection

Date: ___________________________

Current energy level: ☹ 🙁 😐 🙂 😊

I am grateful for:

____

____

____

____

____

____

____

My empowering affirmation:

____

____

____

____

Three things I will do for self-care:

1. ___________________________________

2. ___________________________________

3. ___________________________________

My intention for today:

____

____

____

____

Three goals for the day:

1. _______________________________
   ____
2. _______________________________
   ____
3. _______________________________
   ____

Evening self-reflection:

____
____
____
____
____
____
____
____
____
____
____
____
____
____
____
____
____
____
____

Completed:

☐ Gratitude   ☐ Intention
☐ Affirmation   ☐ Goals
☐ Self-Care   ☐ Self-Reflection

Date: ___________________________

Current energy level: ☹ ☹ 😐 🙂 😊

I am grateful for:

____
____
____
____
____
____
____
____

My empowering affirmation:

____
____
____
____

Three things I will do for self-care:

   1. _______________________________
   2. _______________________________
   3. _______________________________

My intention for today:

____
____
____

Three goals for the day:

1. ___________________________________

   ____

2. ___________________________________

   ____

3. ___________________________________

   ____

Evening self-reflection:

____

____

____

____

____

____

____

____

____

____

____

____

____

____

____

____

Completed:

☐ Gratitude   ☐ Intention
☐ Affirmation   ☐ Goals
☐ Self-Care   ☐ Self-Reflection

Date: _______________________

Current energy level: ☹ 🙁 😐 🙂 😊

I am grateful for:

____
____
____
____
____
____
____
____

My empowering affirmation:

____
____
____
____

Three things I will do for self-care:

1. _________________________________
2. _________________________________
3. _________________________________

My intention for today:

____
____
____
____

Three goals for the day:

1. _______________________

2. _______________________

3. _______________________

Evening self-reflection:

Completed:

- ☐ Gratitude
- ☐ Affirmation
- ☐ Self-Care
- ☐ Intention
- ☐ Goals
- ☐ Self-Reflection

Date: _______________________

Current energy level: ☹ ☹ 😐 🙂 😊

I am grateful for:

____
____
____
____
____
____
____
____

My empowering affirmation:

____
____
____
____

Three things I will do for self-care:

1. ___________________________________
2. ___________________________________
3. ___________________________________

My intention for today:

____
____
____
____

Three goals for the day:

1. _______________________________

2. _______________________________

3. _______________________________

Evening self-reflection:

Completed:

- ☐ Gratitude
- ☐ Affirmation
- ☐ Self-Care
- ☐ Intention
- ☐ Goals
- ☐ Self-Reflection

Date: ________________________

Current energy level: ☹ ☹ 😐 🙂 😊

I am grateful for:

____

____

____

____

____

____

____

____

My empowering affirmation:

____

____

____

____

Three things I will do for self-care:

1. ______________________________________

2. ______________________________________

3. ______________________________________

My intention for today:

____

____

____

____

Three goals for the day:

1. _______________________________
____
2. _______________________________
____
3. _______________________________
____

Evening self-reflection:

____

Completed:

- [ ] Gratitude
- [ ] Affirmation
- [ ] Self-Care
- [ ] Intention
- [ ] Goals
- [ ] Self-Reflection

Date: ________________________

Current energy level: ☹ ☹ 😐 🙂 😊

I am grateful for:

____
____
____
____
____
____
____

My empowering affirmation:

____
____
____
____

Three things I will do for self-care:

1. ____________________________________
2. ____________________________________
3. ____________________________________

My intention for today:

____
____
____

Three goals for the day:

1. _______________________
2. _______________________
3. _______________________

Evening self-reflection:

Completed:

- ☐ Gratitude
- ☐ Affirmation
- ☐ Self-Care
- ☐ Intention
- ☐ Goals
- ☐ Self-Reflection

Date: _______________________

Current energy level: ☹ ☹ 😐 🙂 😊

I am grateful for:

____
____
____
____
____
____
____
____

My empowering affirmation:

____
____
____
____

Three things I will do for self-care:

1. ____________________________________
2. ____________________________________
3. ____________________________________

My intention for today:

____
____
____
____

Three goals for the day:

1. ______________________________________
____
2. ______________________________________
____
3. ______________________________________
____

Evening self-reflection:

____
____
____
____
____
____
____
____
____
____
____
____
____
____
____
____
____
____

Completed:

- [ ] Gratitude
- [ ] Affirmation
- [ ] Self-Care
- [ ] Intention
- [ ] Goals
- [ ] Self-Reflection

Date: _______________

Current energy level: ☹ ☹ ☺ ☺ ☺

I am grateful for:

____
____
____
____
____
____
____
____

My empowering affirmation:

____
____
____
____

Three things I will do for self-care:

1. _______________________________________
2. _______________________________________
3. _______________________________________

My intention for today:

____
____
____
____

Three goals for the day:

1. _______________________________
____
2. _______________________________
____
3. _______________________________
____

Evening self-reflection:

____
____
____
____
____
____
____
____
____
____
____
____
____
____
____
____
____
____

Completed:

- [ ] Gratitude
- [ ] Affirmation
- [ ] Self-Care
- [ ] Intention
- [ ] Goals
- [ ] Self-Reflection

Date: _______________________________

Current energy level: ☹ ☹ 😐 🙂 😊

I am grateful for:

____
____
____
____
____
____
____
____

My empowering affirmation:

____
____
____
____

Three things I will do for self-care:

1. ____
2. ____
3. ____

My intention for today:

____
____
____
____

Three goals for the day:

1. _______________________________

2. _______________________________

3. _______________________________

....

Evening self-reflection:

____

Completed:

☐ Gratitude   ☐ Intention
☐ Affirmation   ☐ Goals
☐ Self-Care   ☐ Self-Reflection

Date: ________________

Current energy level: ☹ ☹ 😐 🙂 😊

I am grateful for:

____
____
____
____
____
____
____
____

My empowering affirmation:

____
____
____
____

Three things I will do for self-care:

1. ____
2. ____
3. ____

My intention for today:

____
____
____
____

Three goals for the day:

1. _______________________________
2. _______________________________
3. _______________________________

Evening self-reflection:

Completed:

- [ ] Gratitude
- [ ] Affirmation
- [ ] Self-Care
- [ ] Intention
- [ ] Goals
- [ ] Self-Reflection

Date: _______________________

Current energy level: ☹ ☹ 😐 🙂 😊

I am grateful for:

____
____
____
____
____
____
____
____

My empowering affirmation:

____
____
____
____

Three things I will do for self-care:

1. ____________________________________
2. ____________________________________
3. ____________________________________

My intention for today:

____
____
____
____

Three goals for the day:

1. __________________________________
   ____
2. __________________________________
   ____
3. __________________________________
   ____

Evening self-reflection:

____
____
____
____
____
____
____
____
____
____
____
____
____
____
____
____
____
____

Completed:

- [ ] Gratitude
- [ ] Affirmation
- [ ] Self-Care
- [ ] Intention
- [ ] Goals
- [ ] Self-Reflection

Date: _______________________

Current energy level: ☹ ☹ 😐 🙂 😊

I am grateful for:

____
____
____
____
____
____
____
____

My empowering affirmation:

____
____
____
____

Three things I will do for self-care:

1. ____
2. ____
3. ____

My intention for today:

____
____
____
____

Three goals for the day:

1. _______________________________
____
2. _______________________________
____
3. _______________________________
____

Evening self-reflection:

____
____
____
____
____
____
____
____
____
____
____
____
____
____
____
____
____
____

Completed:

☐ Gratitude   ☐ Intention
☐ Affirmation   ☐ Goals
☐ Self-Care   ☐ Self-Reflection

Date: _______________________

Current energy level: 🙁 🙁 😐 🙂 😊

I am grateful for:

____
____
____
____
____
____
____

My empowering affirmation:

____
____
____
____

Three things I will do for self-care:

1. ____________________________
2. ____________________________
3. ____________________________

My intention for today:

____
____
____
____

Three goals for the day:

1. _______________________________
____
2. _______________________________
____
3. _______________________________
____

Evening self-reflection:

Completed:

- ☐ Gratitude
- ☐ Affirmation
- ☐ Self-Care
- ☐ Intention
- ☐ Goals
- ☐ Self-Reflection

Date: ___________________________

Current energy level: ☹ ☹ 😐 🙂 😊

I am grateful for:

____

____

____

____

____

____

____

____

My empowering affirmation:

____

____

____

____

Three things I will do for self-care:

1. _________________________________

2. _________________________________

3. _________________________________

My intention for today:

____

____

____

____

Three goals for the day:

1. _______________________________

2. _______________________________

3. _______________________________

Evening self-reflection:

Completed:

☐ Gratitude ☐ Intention

☐ Affirmation ☐ Goals

☐ Self-Care ☐ Self-Reflection

Date: _______________________

Current energy level: ☹ ☹ 😐 🙂 😊

I am grateful for:

____
____
____
____
____
____
____

My empowering affirmation:

____
____
____
____

Three things I will do for self-care:

   1. ___________________________________
   2. ___________________________________
   3. ___________________________________

My intention for today:

____
____
____
____

Three goals for the day:

1. _______________________________
____
2. _______________________________
____
3. _______________________________
____

Evening self-reflection:

Completed:

- [ ] Gratitude
- [ ] Affirmation
- [ ] Self-Care
- [ ] Intention
- [ ] Goals
- [ ] Self-Reflection

Date: _______________

Current energy level: ☹ ☹ 😐 ☺ 😊

I am grateful for:

____
____
____
____
____
____
____

My empowering affirmation:

____
____
____
____

Three things I will do for self-care:

1. ___________________________________
2. ___________________________________
3. ___________________________________

My intention for today:

____
____
____
____

Three goals for the day:

1. _______________________________
____
2. _______________________________
____
3. _______________________________
____

Evening self-reflection:

____
____
____
____
____
____
____
____
____
____
____
____
____
____
____
____
____
____

Completed:

- [ ] Gratitude
- [ ] Affirmation
- [ ] Self-Care
- [ ] Intention
- [ ] Goals
- [ ] Self-Reflection

Date: _______________________

Current energy level: ☹ ☹ 😐 🙂 😊

I am grateful for:

____
____
____
____
____
____
____

My empowering affirmation:

____
____
____
____

Three things I will do for self-care:

1. ____________________________________
2. ____________________________________
3. ____________________________________

My intention for today:

____
____
____
____

Three goals for the day:

1. ______________________________

2. ______________________________

3. ______________________________

Evening self-reflection:

Completed:

- [ ] Gratitude
- [ ] Affirmation
- [ ] Self-Care
- [ ] Intention
- [ ] Goals
- [ ] Self-Reflection

Date: ___________________________

Current energy level: ☹ ☹ 😐 🙂 😊

I am grateful for:

____
____
____
____
____
____
____

My empowering affirmation:

____
____
____
____

Three things I will do for self-care:

1. ______________________________________
2. ______________________________________
3. ______________________________________

My intention for today:

____
____
____
____

Three goals for the day:

1. ___________________________________
   ____
2. ___________________________________
   ____
3. ___________________________________
   ____

Evening self-reflection:

Completed:

- ☐ Gratitude
- ☐ Affirmation
- ☐ Self-Care
- ☐ Intention
- ☐ Goals
- ☐ Self-Reflection

Date: ________________

Current energy level: ☹ ☹ 😐 🙂 😀

I am grateful for:

____
____
____
____
____
____
____

My empowering affirmation:

____
____
____
____

Three things I will do for self-care:

1. ____________________________________
2. ____________________________________
3. ____________________________________

My intention for today:

____
____
____
____

Three goals for the day:

1. ______________________________

____

2. ______________________________

____

3. ______________________________

____

Evening self-reflection:

____
____
____
____
____
____
____
____
____
____
____
____
____
____
____
____
____
____

Completed:

- ☐ Gratitude
- ☐ Affirmation
- ☐ Self-Care
- ☐ Intention
- ☐ Goals
- ☐ Self-Reflection

Connect with Vanessa Marie Dewsbury

vanessamariedewsbury@gmail.com

Instagram: @simplejournals.ca

Sharing is caring!

Share a picture of your Simple Journal on social media and tag us @simplejournals.ca

Check out Vanessa's books on Amazon

Heart Is Where The Home Is

Majestic Reflections

For more information on Simple Journals, please visit www.simplejournals.ca

Notes: